TEE FRANCIS

Sherbet Lemons

First Published in 2019
by
Tee Francis

ISBN - 978-1-910061-61-9

Jacket Design and Typography by
Michelle Collin

www.feelwrite.co.uk

TABLE OF CONTENTS

NAN

And I didn't know it then, but you saved me.
Wrapped in a mist of Impulse
whisky and stale cigarettes,
you permeate my thoughts
in the stillness
when my skin is shed—
that's when I feel
your squeeze expelling my breath
and with it
any doubt
that I am not loved.

HARLOW'S MONKEY

Cage mother, did you know
that you were made of wire?
Hollow.
I tried to love you—
hold you cold and barbed
against my newborn skin,
soft as a shelled egg's membrane,
torn and paper thin.

You abandoned me.
Blinded by panic and an August sun,
I hollered to your shrinking silhouette.
Barefoot on tarmac, burning,
this toddler tried to run.
But cage mothers do not hear.
You refused to turn.

You disappeared
down an alley separating
unfamiliar houses.
I followed into the dark chill
then out into the light of a garden blazing.
The terror of a pylon
black-legged against the sky,
crackling against the white of panic.
Then, your steel legs
finally static.

CIRSIUM HETEROPHYLLUM
(MELANCHOLY THISTLE)

You will find me where the wild flowers grow.
The self-pollinators
aside the trampled path,
not sown in tended fertile beds
as the jonquils,
birthing bulbs
under sun-soaked soil.

From the wasteland I watch them
herald the queen of the narcissi,
basking in reflected golden glory,
then stem the loss
with a single
posthumous
thistle.

PARTS

When I was five, I collided
with the edge of a metal door,
gashed my forehead, required stitches.

On removal, the nurse placed them in
a vial with a lilac-covered lid,
spider-black threads stuck to fragments of skin.

I asked to keep them. Took them home.
Being brave was easy in hospital,
the nurse smiled, said I was, so.

When I was ten, I found my milk teeth
in my mother's jewellery box. A hard
enamel-coloured case that snapped

open and shut on a zealous hinge.
Two sets. My brother's teeth mixed
with mine, smiled jointly without consent.

When I was fifty-two my dentist levered
my Upper Right 6. It resisted. My dribbling mouth
forced wide, it sensed enough parts had been lifted.

ON WALKING TO FLEET CHURCH

We trod the ancient coastal path
warm-baked on an April Sunday.
Felt the thud of our feet lay down
the desk-bound work of a digital week.
Swung the wind-worn kissing gate,
The Fleet stretched out its long sand arm,
held us close in the glistening heat.

Oystercatchers, egrets and terns
stalked the Chesil Beach lagoon
while we turned driftwood, shells and thoughts.
In peace, we walked to the small stone church,
ushered in by field-spun larks; the grassland
laced with fritillaries and bees.
We communed in the blessing of this day,
exhaled our praise into the breeze.

REMOTE CONTROL

Your tongue caressed
through keys and texts,
licked and flicked.
Clitoral connect by internet.
Your mouth hovered warm
over musical hairs
on my top lip.
That pause
before we tasted skin
promised by unsteady breath.
Tapped words whispered
to waiting flesh.

SLOTS
(SPOKEN WORD)

He saw her in the corner of the bar,
swaggered over.
The silverback with a pint of lager
hanging from his palm.
She always welcomed him back.
A quickie could do no harm.

She lit up for him, put on a show.
Her cherries were ripe for plucking.
His low-slung denim pocket was bulging.
A chance, up close and personal.
Primal stance.
His sweaty hands were groping.

She knew how to tease, how to reel him in.
He knew which buttons to press—
no caress—a smash and grab raid
but she was playing hard to get,
she knew he'd just been paid.

Desperate now, he thrust
in his hard-earned gold, felt fully alive
heady with fruit—hold—hold—
stimulation overdrive
ready for the cash shot
he was gonna loot the jackpot.
Cherries were gonna flow
he would plunder all her charms,
he would thrust his hands below,
feel her come in his cupped palms.

A PLACE IN THE SUN
(SPOKEN WORD)

I'm in my villa, Orihuela, drinking lager not Sangria.
I'm an expat, and proud of that, basking on the
Costa Blanca.
No paella, I'm a fella that likes steak, my cake, and eat it.
Speak the lingo? Why? We've bingo, karaoke, bowls
and cricket.

That foreign shit— have none of it, we don't like integrating,
we've banished all the Spanish, find their culture irritating.
We're British, let me finish, all those Spaniards should
be grateful:
we've built over Fuengirola, we've put food upon
their table.

In my man-cave, in this enclave, I watch Top Gear
on repeat,
tried to shake off British Bake Off but I gotta keep
Babs sweet.
It's no longer Chipping Ongar but with satellite TV
It feels like home, without the gays or need to be PC.

We've got PG Tips and Cheddar, but it's better, we've
got sunshine,
eat alfresco, miss our Tesco, but there's gammon, chips
and cheap wine.
We've retired here, got free health-care, English shops
in Alicante—
no hijab-wearing foreigners or Poles in every taxi.

Brown as leather, never better, all the people are our sort.
Voted Brexit cos we're scared shit that they'll over-run
our ports—
I'm not racist but let's face it, we need to take control back
from those bureaukrauts in Brussels, and make the bloody
lot pack.

'Hypocrisy?' Democracy! We want our country OUT.
The irony is lost on me? — What are you on about?
I'm sick of this, get on with it, make Britain great again,
let's have order, close the borders, but me? I'll stay
in Spain.

ODE TO JEREMY HUNT
(SPOKEN WORD)

Jeremy Hunt, what a shame
the BMA are not to blame
you give staff and patients hell
with NHS on your lapel.
You anaesthetise us through the press
with soundbites on the NHS
then defecate on low achievers
rashly thinking we believe that
care is better privatised;
life-line services monetised.

Jeremy Hunt, rhymes with this
a place synonymous with bliss;
birth, life and sanctuary,
motherhood and maternity.
Nurturing and caring, I guess
which is just like our NHS—
not you, the posh child, giving suck
who truly couldn't give a fuck
for while you smirk in shirts of silk
you asset-strip our mother's milk.

Jeremy Hunt, what a country
this is now, to put it bluntly:
a class-based cleansing epidemic,
poverty policies are endemic;
eugenics, social engineering;
as a nation we are veering
to a state where being healthy
is a privilege for the wealthy.
All the while you sneer and lie,
vulnerable, trusting people die.

FORBIDDEN PLEASURE
(SPOKEN WORD)

I have a dirty secret. Well, actually it's clean.
I do something in the bathroom which some might
deem obscene.
I'd do it in your bathroom, too, if conditions were conducive.
I've tried to get help for this but support groups
prove elusive.
The act itself is not lewd, it's the fact it gives me pleasure,
so the scale of my depravity is very hard to measure.
I take a household item, freely sold throughout the nation
and purposely employ it for my self-gratification.

I engage in
aural sex. That's aural with 'a-u'
and do things with a cotton bud you really should not do.
My ear-holes are not waxy, but when in the vicinity
of a stash of pure white cotton buds, I lose my ear virginity.
I feel like Pavlov's dog on heat, not turned on by a bell—
a tub of Johnson's cotton buds is my aurotic hell:
before I know what's happening, I'm clasping in my fingers
a three-inch wand that's heading for my auditory meatus.

Just Google ears and cotton buds, you'll see I'm not alone
in abusing this erogenous, neglected sensual zone.
It's such a simple pleasure, can it really be a sin
if your Q tips are hygienic and disposed of in a bin?

I feel such shame indulging in auricular stimulation
but it's not something I'd introduce in bedtime
conversation,
we've tried bondage, fruit, outdoor 'pursuits',
spray cream, but I feel it's
a step too far to ask him if he'd lick my antihelix
or tantalise my tragus with a feather or a finger;
to whisper in my ear canal, my concha or my pinna.

But now a word of caution, and I hope I make this clear:
manufacturers forbid you to put buds inside your ear,
but if you cannot help yourself, and share in my depravity,
if you spend time with Q-tips swirling round your
aural cavity,
don't do it multi-tasking, keep your safety to the fore,
don't do it walking down the stairs to open the front door.
There is a risk of danger which may add a certain frisson,
but too much penetration and you'll perforate your
ear drum.
Don't let children see you, please, make sure the door
is closed;
don't try another orifice, especially not your nose!
And think of the environment; the situation's drastic,
So, friends, if you must do this, please avoid those made
with plastic.

HYMN FOR HIM

When the tip of your flesh touches mine
stars melt at the back of my eyes
my skin sings silent hymns
my life-blood flows like wine.
Then I want to live inside you
surge through your aching limbs
to be your breath, your heartbeat
until our twilight dims.

SHARK BAIT

The lipstick was her mistake.
Red lips gasped for attention.
Torn petals on a turbulent sea
mouthed silently for breath.

He directed her knife
as she cut and spread
crimson meat on curling bread,
his smiling mouth unstrung
from eyes that pierced the blue,
like a dorsal fin slices through
the pause before death.

She replaced the knife.
Offered her soul, on a plate, in sacrifice
to the shark-god hooked on jugular blood.
She felt the tug on her wretched life.
Waited for her lungs to flood.

ON LEAVING PORTSMOUTH

Gridlocked isle of my defence
you sheltered me from
French-based threats,
by the Solent, not your ships.
Great hulks of grey with glorious names:
Invincible and Sir Galahad
moored in time-lines, a fine line
between naval might
and scrap.

Hidden behind the Isle of Wight
we're refugees, you and I,
based on this flat gem:
Landport, Buckland
Fratton, North End.

Where no-one asked my history,
accepted me along with all
the takeaways, tattooists,
Poundland clones and Polish shops,
The thousand Aqua Cars that mooch
beneath the Pompey tower blocks.
A post-war concrete legacy,
Pickwick House and Copperfield
a nod to Dickens' residency.
There's no Bleak House ironically.

Any port in a storm,
Portsmouth, my port.
My storm now weathered
it's time to move on.
Untether my life,
up-anchor, get gone.
I've been salvaged.

Battle-scarred
from PO1

SILENT TREATMENT

He listened—
truly listened and before we met
for coffee I was sewn to him.
Hooked through an April night with empathy.
Words that vibrated the core of me.
Hydrated, penetrated,
resuscitated.

All night we typed—
laughed at YouTube links,
he played Stay with me till Dawn
it sounds corny, but I did.

Our eyes paired through coffee steam.
Fingers brushed—
a high voltage touch
that left me clean.

I watch you wake,
fold in to kiss your silent ears.
Your body listens to mine,
hands find me, fingers entwine
then, smiling, you sign:
I love you.

COMMUNION

Did I stir your twilight blue
or call you in the pause of dawn?
With whispered touch, my tongue incline
to breathe my temple, mould my spine
like warm dough on your supine form?
Still wearing my essential dew
submerged in slumber, softly roused.
Tousled hair beneath my lips,
the hunger of a moment shared,
momentum of magnetic hips.

To fuel our fire
we stopped the earth from breathing
in our airless dark.
Nature's vital life-force stolen.
Flesh-consuming, swooning, swollen.
Asphyxiated, melting thighs;
my siren howling out the brink—
we die, flames quenched in fluid spent.
Our eyes in total
blissful sync.

NEW SHOOTS

This February morning
I shuffled into the conservatory
trying to face the day
in dressing gown, clasping coffee
and noticed
the tiny potted Christmas tree
I had watered intermittently
not wanting to invest too much hope
in its survival past New Year
had sprouted
six or seven shoots
of the newest green:
perfect miniature needles
that danced and sparkled
in my joyful bauble tears.

SYNTHETICS

Programme for delicates:
A thirty-seven degree drumroll
for the dirty words that tumble
like a Hotpoint on rinse.

Rinsing is a solitary cycle:
soiled memories privately laundered.
Resentment rotated with a dose
of spring-fresh fabric conditioner.

A smell to hide a smell
is not recommended by experts,
but may bring lasting freshness
for up to seven days.

CHOCOLATE GODS

Where are you Jesus,
our Father, this Easter?
Sunday strewn with Cadbury foil
and billions with a belly-full
of sugar-coated pills.

I search for bulletins
of rebirth and hope, but
flounder in Fake news,
bombarded by suffering;
the Mother of all Bombs and
chocolate cake to die for.

BATTERY FARMING

We stacked them in cages
rack upon rack
their cages charred black
by the cladding that rages.
Lungs hushed in ash
cremated en masse
the poor and the nameless
traded for cash.
Austerity's blameless.
Only now Grenfell's flameless
do we speak of inspection
evacuation, regulation.
Your Red Tape initiative,
your think tanks,
your blood banks
made sprinklers prohibitive.
Our parliament members
who govern our safety
are landlords who watched
tenants turn into embers for profit.
Now, in commemoration,
this nation must sound the alarm
not legislate harm or factory farm
the vulnerable in our population.

THE DEATH OF T. REX

I was roped into dutiful daughter at your bedside.
You made small talk while the nurse in plastic apron
took an age to check your connections
but not the twenty years you took.
You said you were sorry—
easy words to say but not swallow.
Time too short to catalogue cruelty,
besides, propriety shields the dying.

My forgiveness dutifully given, you died the next day
without having seen your grandchildren grow up.

At your funeral, my brother and I sat at the back
watching those who knew you less
extol your virtues and cry.
We wondered if they spoke of the same man.
They didn't know you clubbed a sheep to death
or burned the dog on pallets when she died.

Your plywood, stapled coffin
hovered to Eric Clapton.
Sanctity in death.
All sins Febrezed by God
and the priest you gave a lift to in the rain.
Your next choice of song: Metal Guru
ruined for me now, you selfish bastard.

They threw flowers in your grave.
I threw a snotty tissue and my brother walked off.
We wanted no part in your circus.
Goodbye, Dad. Rest in peace, why don't you.

INSOMNIA

Quell your joy-notes, blackbird
for the faint, first breath of light.
I've held my lover, Darkness,
through unconsummated night.
Wait till slumber seals my lids,
till dreams float me away,
then adorn your precious morn
and greet presumptuous day.

LEGACY

They gave me the sapphire earrings
that you died in:
miniscule midnight stones
I'd bought on low wages;
a present for your birthday,
you loved them, wore them always.
But I couldn't wear them—
couldn't bear the thought of you
bird-like, lying there.

But your hair, from my scalp, grows wild.
Stubborn grizzly curls
that made me grimace as a child
but I've grown to love them in time,
to embrace the springy ringlets
that fizz around my face,
all the coarse, wiry strands.
Now, as I wind them
or coax them back into place,
I feel your love coiled
In my grateful hands.

WITH GRATITUDE

This book is dedicated to the people in my life who have made a difference. I would particularly like to thank Fred Sedgwick, my primary school teacher, who shared his love of poetry and inspired me to write; to Kim Miles for being a steadfast friend for over forty years; to Paul Canon Harris, for believing in my poetry when I didn't, and to the other support networks who have encouraged and supported me: John and Becky, Apothecary regulars, Michael and Sally Forte, Claire Williamson, Fiona Hamilton, Nigel Gibbons, Graham Harthill and my Metanoia sisters: Cath, Lizzie, Marie, and Sarah.

Lily, Alfie and Adi, I love you more than I can possibly express. Thank you for your unfailing love, support and encouragement.

I would also like to dedicate this book to the memory of my nan, Kathleen Rance, who was a vital beacon of love and touch in an abusive, neglectful childhood. I love you more than all the tea in China.

ABOUT THE AUTHOR

Tee Francis is a poet and writer, based in Dorset. She regularly performs her poetry in the South West and co-hosts the Apothecary spoken word night in Bridport. She studied at the Metanoia Institute, London, and has an MSc in Creative Writing for Therapeutic Purposes. She facilitates writing and poetry workshops and has a particular interest in the use of poetry, journaling and creativity for self-development; to overcome procrastination; and as a valuable resource to navigate complex PTSD, chronic illness, and child abuse.

She is passionate about the environment, enjoys live music, a good bargain, gardening, wine-making and foraging. She has mad hair, three kidneys and a serious stationery addiction.

Tee Francis may be contacted via her website:
www.feelwrite.co.uk

www.ingramcontent.com/pod-product-compliance
Lightning Source LLC
Chambersburg PA
CBHW020443030426
42337CB00014B/1378